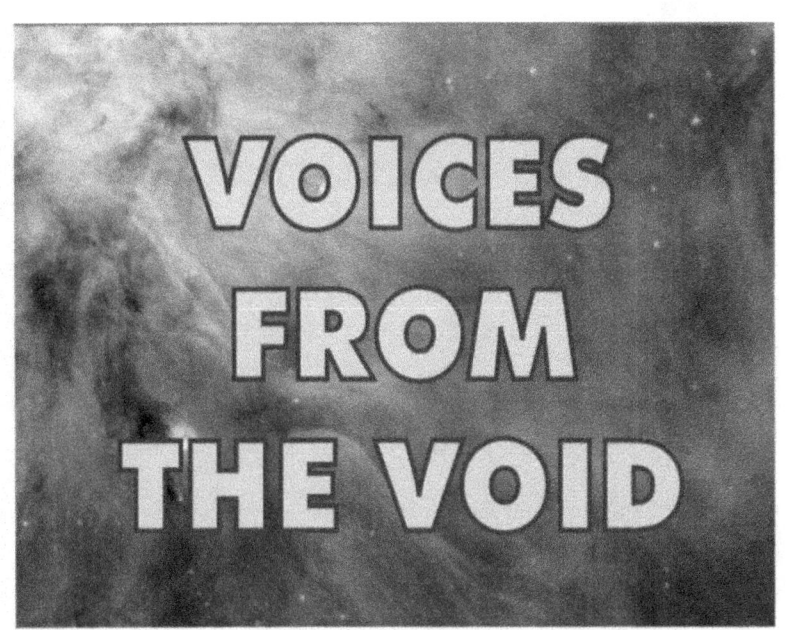

VOICES FROM THE VOID

POEMS & PROSE-POEMS

THOMAS D. JONES

The Poet's Press
PITTSBURGH, PA

Copyright © 2008 by Thomas D. Jones
All Rights Reserved
Second Edition, 2019

Book design by Brett Rutherford
Cover photo from Hubble Telescope,
NASA

This is the 238th publication of
THE POET'S PRESS
2209 Murray Avenue #3
Pittsburgh, PA 15217
ISBN 978-0-922558-98-8
www.poetspress.org

This book is also published in
Adobe Acrobat (PDF) format.

CONTENTS

COSMIC
    On Independence Day   13
    Background   14
    When I Have Fears That I May Live Forever   15
    Life of a Bean   16
    Order of Things   17
    Stargazer   18
    Siegfried's Sword   19
    Visions of Mortality   21
    Life As It Is   22
    Not A Public Way   23
    Frontier Life   24
    Spring Song in Winter   26

EXISTENTIAL
    An Old House   29
    A Bagger's Life   30
    Nikolai   32
    The Blind Teacher   33
    Many Names   34
    September 11, 2001   35
    Rest Stop   37
    Latin Singer   38
    Moon Shadows   40
    To a Moon Child   42

IMAGINATIVE
    Flute Girl   45
    Shaman's Stone (20,000 Years Ago)   47
    Slaying the Minotaur   50
    "Every day more bombings in Cairo,
       near the Pyramids, under the eyes
       of the Sphinx   51

Hope for Relief   53
Illusion   54
Your Worst Nightmare   55
Reply from a Prophet   57
Palm Reading   59
Sun Spots   61
Solar Night   63
Song to Imagination   65
Doctor P...   67

NARRATIVE
Four Visions of the Muse   71
M.B.   75
Tithonous in Modern Times,
    Human and Grasshopper   77
Maiden Tree: A Pastoral   80
Monster's Revenge   84
Footprints   86
Loss   88
Deadpan Alley   89

NONSENSICAL
Singer   93
Skyfall   94
Lament in Summer   95
Day at the Circus   97
Hurdy-gurdy   99
Phantom   100
To Poets Who Would Be Fastidious   101
Fragment   102

POLITICAL
    Company Knee   105
    Last Rites   107
    Fear of Sorcerers Spurs Killings in Java (Indonesia)   109

AMOROUS
    Suzette   113
    China Doll   114
    Rosa   115
    Love Song   116
    If I Have Love   117
    Pineapple Lovers   118
    Love Language   119
    Once Loved   120
    When Opening the Book, You Will See This: 122

ABOUT THE AUTHOR   123

VOICES FROM THE VOID

To Rosa, my love, my wife

COSMIC

ON INDEPENDENCE DAY

A raptor takes the shape of a flag
spread across the top of my house.
Is this the same creature who soars majestic
in mid-air? Smaller, it stands wild, untamed,
unruly, not guardian-wise, nor invincible.
Relieved, I hear a neighbor call it hawk,
for eagles soar with too much majesty
and responsibility, suffer too much burden,
the weight of the sky on their shoulders. Hawks carry
only their own spirit through time and space,
scrappy, clawing their way through rough terrain,
and dive headstrong after their prey
despite the cost, the chance to fail and fall.

BACKGROUND

Look at yourself in the mirror, the ridges
and cracks of your body
pumiced through years of exertion;
shaped by the flow of Time,
like the water, the scraps and debris
that scrape and scratch and wear down
to mica spots, diamond chips, meteor powder,
moon sand and desert dust, microbes
of matter half alive and half dead,
unseen energy clouds, atoms, motions
of starlight below the visible spectrum,
the moment you crumble, erased from memory,
when people speak of you as "was,"
and the last bit of you floats somewhere
out in the endless dark.

WHEN I HAVE FEARS
THAT I MAY LIVE FOREVER

When I have fears that I may live forever,
this mortal coil never sloughed off flesh,
like books that never leave a teeming brain,
I know from much experience and pain
how traces of my shadow on the wall
and remnants of my former self
become atomic dust and particles.
Though love, I hope, outlasts the end of time,
I know that I shall look no more upon
the people whom I love, but instead will see
their flesh melt to skull, socket, shoulder blade,
the flame burn bright and then expire down to dust.
When I have fears that I may live forever,
I feel flesh and frame break down and sever.

LIFE OF A BEAN

Only the brave eat beans,
the brazen break them with utensils
or between teeth; squirt the brine,
sweet milky-way bubble brew,
breast milk of an infant ancestor
whose ghost broods, breaches, bursts
a bearded body into light from the dust
of the grave, a billion stars
and the big bang, the baby in the crib.

The new soul will sing of the beauty
of long-dead lovers; in bliss embrace
the elements, the seasons, crest and trough,
the motions of the earth and waves;
brace for the day when people,
objects, and life bonds blur,
break away, blown by the breath
of breaking wind to breed
in another body
after digesting beans.

ORDER OF THINGS

Nobody ever said this teeming thing
called life would be gliding
over smooth stone, waiting for ripples
in the lake to clear or waves in the ocean
to lose their white hair, water to run
between coral and stone, into a shallow pool.
Nobody told us, naked and fearful,
screaming out from the water,
dumb brutes in need of discipline,
put here to scrape the scraps,
what little made for ourselves,
like all other animals
seeking a niche or a specialty
marked above the rest, only to find
another more gifted or clever.
Nobody prepared us for nights of despair,
oblivion, self-destruction, emptiness,
insanity, unrequited love, and loss of friends.
Even if we hold our dear ones next to us,
be they animal or human, our thoughts
will interfere with our being
and we will be constant mendicants
who seek a place in the order of things
with none above to trample us.

STARGAZER

When I see stars through the window,
I feel liquid emotion, starstuff
burning in the heart of a nebula,
iron and granite spinning around me,
my body a flaming ocean.

Mountains of flame, like fingers,
rise from each pole to scorch
some planets, warm others
and leave others in the cold.
I am not like them, the planets
who wander. I occupy the center.

I will burn yellow for eons,
then become bloated and red,
red vein, red pulse, red ocean,
and eat the planets nearest me,
rejoined with atoms billions of years old.

Like an aging star losing energy,
I too will explode to supernova,
destroy the last planets in cinders,
a dragon from the myths of old
who expels a final fire-gasp.

In a gap of improbable years,
I will implode into a hole in space,
invisible till entered, dense and deep,
an ocean immense and eternal,
no particles escaping my maelstrom.

SIEGFRIED'S SWORD

As the dwarf connives to take my life,
I forge anew my father's sword,
the sword which broke on Wotan's spear.

I hammer from the smithy oven
with the sound of ping ping ping.
grab the ring, get the ring!

Again the sound, ping ping ping,
reach the ground and hear it sing,
"Heigh-ho Heigh-ho!"
"Blow, blow on the blaze!"

It smelts the splinters of the soul,
it builds a new sword out of old.
"Heigh-ho Heigh-ho!"

I am the one with all the power,
I am the one who grows in strength,
I am the one to take the day!
"Blow and blaze away!"

I come to claim my father's sword,
and take evil from the world.
I have no fear and no remorse,
I can change the evil course.

Grab the ring, get the ring,
kill the dragon of my fear!

With stout blows I'll beat you straight,
and make all fear shrink away.
Soon upon the world I'll go,
and kill the dragon Fafner.

I build a sword out of the fire,
and take away all cowardice.
"Heigh-ho Heigh-ho!"

VISIONS OF MORTALITY

How do you feel over an abyss?
Loved ones encircled around you
to play a dirge for your soul?
You shake your head and look away,
but turn to look again.

You think about the glory won and lost,
the game played well but still destroyed.
As escape, you climb a world mountain
to wrestle with your statue,
an alter-ego brushed away in wind.

The pain comes in looking down to find
the secure bed gone, the splintered house,
the room of youth now ravaged, dissolved
in the quest to make a living and a name.

Inquisitive Job, you ask of God,
"How long will suffering continue?"
Or is misery which appears to you
in the mirror held to your face
of little consequence to teeming stars —

The same bald light in the paradise you lost,
the same carbon, hydrogen, and helium
which burned and blinded all seeing eyes,
the truth a gargoyle apparition to behold.

LIFE AS IT IS

A bird outside improvises a familiar melody,
each song a new strain for the universe.
The sun rises and falls in its course,
each day closer to or further from the earth.
Redwood trees continue to stand and face the sky,
but each day one tree falls out of hearing.
The earth and planets spin a million miles per second,
but no one feels the earth move in its orbit.
The universe itself spins, and is not conscious
of human havoc, of disaster, of lives collapsed to ash.

NOT A PUBLIC WAY

(Seen on a Street Sign)

A private way?
Of the introvert, monk, and muse
A way not taken, less traveled, never considered
A stray cat's tin-pan alley
A place to stay away from
Not part of the plan
Different from the right way
Of the Buddha, the truth, the life,
The woman, the warrior, and the world —
A forgotten path one person takes,
A drug to forget life's troubles,
A key to lock away the heart,
To face death as the rosebud closes.

FRONTIER LIFE

Our journey begins with meager means:
a rocket launched from a pad on earth,
a robot to roam in place of our feet
the sanguine soil and shrines of rock.

What can this mechanical rover
discover in million year old rubble?
Amino acids, the building block,
complex proteins, remnants of water,
soil once teeming with life
now parched by a cold desert?

Few of us live to see
the secrets of a planet unfold
until we send those of our own
to stand, touch, smell, and hear
in their own bodies an alien land.

The aliens we find resemble the blood
of our blood and the flesh of our flesh,
our dreams and aspirations reflected
in the eyes of copper-skinned creatures
with an extra head.

Once a handful of people mine the rocks
for chemical riches, others will follow
ad infinitum to build a better life.
Speaking a tongue not understood,
they become aliens in a foreign land,
the natives all but vanished
or dead from the common cold.

Our people love as on earth,
dream the same dreams
sought in the same cities
with the same problems.
In time the new world feels old
and tired, each day the routine
of going to work, getting and spending,
the same old boon as before.

Soon the new world feels ordinary,
love in the world ordinary,
and the only two people left
will crave each other
after mass annihilation,
and will look to the stars again
together.

SPRING SONG IN WINTER

Spring nymph, come!
Look upon the fields!
Spring nymph, come!
Look upon the waters!
Come, arrive in aspiration,
footfalls across a ballet stage,
a vital pulse in hidden darkness.
Come, spring nymph, come!
in a red raw season,
bring Helios shining light of reason,
crimson with the ancient rose petal,
and bless the lintel of a maiden's house.
Come from beneath snow cliffs,
secret lairs and slumbers.
Draw forth your latent tears
from the tips of dormant grass.
Come on cold hungry days!
Arise from the frozen pool!
Take your place among the lost
in an hour of vanished voices.

EXISTENTIAL

AN OLD HOUSE

Its hull rotting out and creaking,
a decrepit old woman
barely able to move a limb.
What will make it take a fall?
Hurricane? Tornado? Blizzard?

The occupants have read reports of spooks:
the old lady who poisoned her husband,
the shadow in the hall with a broad-axe,
the consumptive who died in his underwear,
and the serial killer who stalked his prey.

One day the house will be a ghost,
its memory in the annals of the lost.
Those who once took a vow to never
let a house die, now live out ends of days
in a newer house made of brick and plaster,
a cheaper solution for a second-rate age,
the character and soul of a trying world.

Though I now live in a home my own,
the old house lurks offstage, out of view,
a reminder of all the months paying rent
when occupants came and went,
and lovers sought to love one last time.

A BAGGER'S LIFE

Plastic or paper?
Double, single, or triple bag?
Don't want it to break; groceries
spill and roll on the floor.
"Double bag only with paper,
careful not to squash the fruit!"
the little old lady
scolds the uniformed bagger.
"Only with paper," he thinks, poems
scribbled in blue on the sides,
each line set into place.

The poet, the bagger, stops for a break,
takes a sandwich from the fridge
and paper from a satchel.
He writes only about what he knows:
how butchers wrap fresh meat,
careful to touch it with gloves
and wrap the plastic around it.
How produce clerks make salad,
mix lettuce, peppers, tomatoes, and olives.
How pharmacists grab pills from the shelf,
count each one with dainty care,
pour the correct dose in the bottle.
How customer service develops pictures,
stacks negatives and positives together.
How bakers display the newest cakes,
the frosting newly spread on the top.

His co-workers think him crazy
to write down dreams between stocking shelves,
to leave little notes in the lettuce patch,
to write on the lids, containers, and cans
of soup, assorted nuts, and coffee grounds.

They catch him writing on huge boxes
of paper towels before getting stacked away.
The poem, like bagging or stocking shelves,
requires focus to get it right:
the cans, the fruit, the frozen dinners,
each one carefully chosen to fit on the shelf,
each handled with care in the bag.

He stares at the customers, grocery laden,
their world apart from his,
each item inching closer and closer,
the pile larger and larger, growing in size.
He grabs each thing off the conveyor
and thinks of a line for his newest poem,
of all the poems he's read,
along with the lettuce, ground beef, chicken breasts,
and pork rinds ever bagged. Each one vanishes
into the bag, but later he pulls out his pad
and records them on paper.

The conveyor moves like a treadmill,
endless with each new customer.
The food people did not kill,
and the vegetables they did not grow
continue mindless toward his hands,
the rhythm hurried with no breath or relief.
The poet turns to the other baggers
who throw each item in the bag
without a thought or concern. He thinks
about going home, about the poems yet to write.

NIKOLAI

Nikolai's shift starts at 10 am.
Nikolai lunches at twelve.
Nikolai's shift ends at 8 pm.
Nikolai goes home to screaming kids.
Nikolai yells at his wife for dinner.

The universe cares nothing for Nikolai.
It keeps rolling along in a giant ball.
Eons have passed before Nikolai
and eons will pass after him.
He will only persist in starstuff.

Nikolai goes to work upset.
Nikolai has a splitting headache.
Nikolai bangs his head on a machine.
Nikolai screams at his boss.
In the age of this planet,
Nikolai hasn't been here long.

The universe cares nothing for Nikolai.
It has no reason; it has no flesh.
It's a monstrous whale which broods
over matter and all that exists.
But it's necessary for Nikolai
to keep moving along
even though he'll soon be dust.

THE BLIND TEACHER

My stick taps in front as I walk
without touching any walls,
without the pain of scraped fingers
against the rough metal locker door.
I need an acute sense not to fall or stop,
to hold my balance and not waver.
I continue to walk the line
with only my stick for a guide.

What I cannot see, I hear:
the least movement of a hand or finger,
a roach on the wall, the buzz of a bee,
a whisper in the courtyard from ill-fated,
ill-starred lovers not yet broken-hearted.

The mere fear of hearing invisible feet
would make the sighted shrink in the corner.
Yet I command attention, clear a path
down the center and push forward,
no matter how much the students twirl me.

Most would walk crooked, zig zag
from locker to locker, from door to door,
and cry for help in a crowded room.
But *my* will is made of concrete,
my mind as clear as a blackboard
to move with purpose, self-directed,
determined to reach the end of the hall.

At the end, I find the classroom,
close the door before the bell,
call the name of unseen students,
and teach their minds to see.

MANY NAMES

The Old One, Jehovah, Yaweh, Shiva, Buddha, Quetzalcoatl, Osiris, Allah, Dionysus, Diana, Hermes, Zeus, Creator, Kali, Pachamama, Inti, Quila, Vishnu, Wotan, War Monger, Peace Lover, Great One, The Universe, The Universal, Quasar, Pulsar, Black Hole, Singularity, All That Is, The One, The Quark, Superstring, Quanta, Great Creator, Great Spirit, Spirit of Life, Father Time, The Old Man in the Sea, The Man in the Moon, Gandalf, The Nameless One, Zero, The Sublime, The Name, The Nameless Name, The Lord God Almighty, The Unknown, The Darkness, The Strange and Wonderful, The All Powerful, Most Merciful, Most Terrible, Most Compassionate, The Transcendental, The Word, Word Up, The Good to Go, The Fall Guy, The Sound, The Soundless Sound, The Presence, Outer Space, Inner Space, The Depths, The Thousands of Miles Below the Surface, The Ineffable, The Incredible Lightness of Being There, The Unmoved Mover, The Uncaused Cause, The...

SEPTEMBER 11, 2001

It came from zero, not from nothing,
not out of nowhere, but in two planes.
The hands which built them
could not have done so without zero,
without a number before number one,
before the concept of a country.
In ages past, Arab astronomers
discovered the universe began with zero,
and charted the heavens with symbols.
The first one looked like an O,
of no consequence to anyone.
The second one looked like a finger.
They added these two together
to give them the number one.

Out of two numbers comes one.
Two people, a male and female,
together make one mind and feeling.
Two houses make one community,
two villages one town, two towns one city,
two cities one state, and two states one country.
The number zero makes it all possible,
as it made possible one plane, then another,
each driven by one pilot.
One plane into the first tower,
the next plane into the second tower.
down, down the towers curled
with the force of Arab mathematics.
Down to the ground, to zero, where it all began
with a Japanese architect using Arab numbers.

Begin again from the ground of zero,
zero, one, two, three, four.
See each floor rebuild to the top,
one by one, step by step, floor by floor.
See the ashes take on shapes again,
see the firemen retreat, see the ground floor
with markets, newsstands, bustling people.
See two people coming up the escalator,
see them walking through the corridors
to the street, to a taxi, to a friend's car.
See the two tourists carrying cameras
and New York paraphernalia.
See two lovers walk toward each other,
see them hold out arms and embrace.
See tourists go to the top, the last stop,
to the flat top where King Kong stood.
All this was brought to you by zero.
Zero giveth and zero taketh away.

REST STOP

I awake with a start,
barely remember last night,
too drunk, too carried away in a daze
by someone with a big smile.
I crawl out of bed to a coffee cup
waiting on the night table.
In a flash I remember last night
as I turned the corner
on the street outside
to look for love but missed it.

Like a dwarf in mirror light,
in the last shred of rain,
I open the door of my motel room
and look beyond cheap walls
at a city still and empty
where time hardly budges an inch.
I look in the parking lot,

at my car parked outside,
at lonesome dead ends
where tinted cars move in procession,
grim faces peer from dirty windows,
and flowers grow through cracks
in asphalt tundra. And the cup
on the motel table holds no drink
to be renewed.

LATIN SINGER

For Mercedes Sosa

On a stage in Argentina,
she sings to a packed hall
of common laborers
who listen for Latina wisdom:
her mellifluous tones a huge bell
whose clapper cannot be silenced
against explosive threats of death,
military clubs, fists, and handcuffs
forced on both audience and singer —
the exile of her bloody body
but the spirit left unbowed.

This vast woman, expanding
like the universe in all its terror,
with passion and intelligence,
sings the multitude of voices
unheard above censorship,
campaign ads, secret police,
and corrupt party leaders.

Her childhood of abject poverty,
ignorance and fear,
vanishes with her voice,
however strange to unaccustomed ears,
and on the heels of jazz or folk
her song rises past Andean hills
to settle in the Rockies or Appalachia,
exile transformed into energy.

Ancient and ageless, she sings
the songs of earth and time,
Ella canta la cancion historical
y internacional:
Babylonian, Egyptian, Grecian,
Mayan, Incan, Andean, Argentine,
until young Mestizo ears burn again
with the passion of Quetzalcoatl
and in anger rebel against
powers that would stop their song.

MOON SHADOWS

Love of men, intensive care,
the heartbeat gone with a glimpse,
the body alone like dust and mold,
parents long since departed,
friends nowhere to be found,
arid pews in the church
you and he attended, old boots
where he hid the coins,

His past life hidden from plain view:
grew up in rural Pennsylvania,
a nerdy boy who got into trouble
later as an adult with drugs and booze,
who took trains late at night
to meet his lovers at rendezvous.

His coins now in your pocket
which you sprinkle in the plate,
plate and coins the shape of wafers,
the host shining like the moon.
The priest hisses when you hesitate
and refuse to let go the coins,
the memory of your friend
on the day you clean up his bed.

After the bed, you open the closet
to find a binder in which you imagine
magic runes filled with ancient secrets.
Like such a book, it slowly removes the veils
he so long hid from your gaze:
the promiscuity, the chronic unemployment,
the turn to religion, the move to New York
where you both work at a major publisher
and share a three bedroom flat.

In the hospital you stare at him:
one eye closed, the other open
as if a surreal painting by Dali or Goya,
the slow disintegration of his body,
the moaning in the room, friends by his side
praying for him in low murmurs.

And you the only one who cares
to visit him as he goes, a nobody,
once a boy, a man, a lover.
And those eyes, those eyes

of Mary staring down at you
from the room, the hospital wall,
the suffering of his eyes
as he refused to die in vain,
though he knew it was over,
the rosary and Eucharist
mixed up in one wild orgy
with the hissing snake and screams.

The boots hurt as you walk home,
the deity, the host, the coins in your pocket,
the memory of the words in his room,
"My strength cometh from the Lord."
Only a talisman appears on your door,
a serpent entwined, a symbol
of caduceus, antidote to poison.
As you enter your room
and move to your bed,
your fingers entwined unwind
as you undress, scatter your clothes,
and pull away the sheets stained
with silver of the moon.

TO A MOON CHILD

You sleep like an animal in snow cave
as the moon floats past your window,
its jagged, white-peaked mountains,
the cold granite shining like snow.
You lie in the bed with eyes closed,
a mouth shut against screams,
unable to speak in any tongue.
The hit and run stopped it for good,
muted your voice in the bed.
My voice bounces from window to moon,
from moon to your window, your bed.
The ancient bell of Buddha tolls
once, twice, thrice, then no more.
I will descend the depths of craters
and float across the valley of shadows
to be with you when your eyes open
and you reach for my arms
in the last shred of moonlight.

IMAGINATIVE

FLUTE GIRL

As her fingers play,
I am drawn into her Inca soul:
The mountain summits, the arid deserts,
cacti in one valley, vegetation in the next,
the stone dwellings carved and smoothed like glass,
each piece fit neatly into place.

In the music her lips conceal
a language of knots and cords
carried by a runner down
the trapezoid mountain fortress
to reach me in the age of machines —
a small room where she sells
Alpaca coats and large earring masks
to tourists who swoop like condors for loot
but who can never dive
into her warm adobe water.

The flute, her voice, the wind
speaks *Inti* — Sun; *Quilla* — Moon,
phallus and breast:
her face like Tupac Amaru's,
last Incan king or princess, androgynous:
long hair like stone polished to glass
with precious herbs and cactus juice.

She plays in honor of the elements,
the Puma resting on the surface
of Pachamama, the embracer,
and in reverence to the sun
who rises over father mountain.

Her body tied to the sun disk,
she welcomes the solstice.
A sudden bright flash appears
in the temple mirror,
fresh flesh ignited by Inti,
swallowed by Puma,
digested in Pachamama's belly
where Snake grinds it to dust
blown on the fluted wind
in the cold mountain night.

SHAMAN'S STONE (20,000 YEARS AGO)

Deep dark
One-eyed giants
Hairy beasts
Long noses
Two white pointed noses
Spears in flesh

Blizzard
Raw
Hands in fire
Hands on fire!
Pain, red flesh
Paint
Walls
Animals
Gods

Mother clothes
Mother food
Mother not here
Men here
Flesh smell in fire
Mm good!

My sons
My daughters
Sweat
The sun
Hot
The sand
Swish
The waves
Wah wah wah
Baby
Gulls

Tomorrow?
Children?
No more children?
Big children!
Man and woman
Man and woman and children
Children
Big children
Man and woman
More children
Many people
Too many people
Many people hurt earth?

Screams, fists
People fall
Up, down,
Blood
Screams, fists
People fall
Up, down,
Blood
Prisoners

Bear hole
Cavern belly
Rug skin
Bum cold
Outside? Inside?
Sun or no sun?
More flames
More people
No more flames
No more people
Light
Big flash!
Night
Big cat noise
Hairy beast cover
Dead noise
Head on stone
Sleep

SLAYING THE MINOTAUR

I look to the center of the carpet,
every weave and bob of the loom,
handspun thread the shape of labyrinth,
the forest of my boyhood hideous and hairy,
the many faces who haunt the magic circle
of the ancestors long since gone under.

I, a pilgrim walking the sacred path,
hear growls from the hidden room
and know the monster stalks fresh prey
in the center where the two meet and clash,
never die, and return to fight again.
At the threshold of this maze I stand,
a Greek hero or a Samurai
taking a breath before the final blow,
playing invincible before the foe
against whom I survive and shake
a fist at the origin of all that is.
When sinking and hopeless,
bitter and broken, I know what keeps
the animal at bay: the choice to stay or leave,
decide against death in the face of all,
and take the monster with me in the fall.

"EVERY DAY MORE BOMBINGS IN CAIRO, NEAR THE PYRAMIDS, UNDER THE EYES OF THE SPHINX"

Some say they have seen a strange creature
creep from a forgotten tomb.
He moans with arms forward and drags
one leg across the ground, rags trailing behind,
making a scraping sound,
his bandaged head face forward
in the moonlight, bathed in the stars.

He waited four thousand years
for a terrorist bomb to grant him liberty
from his prison, where Tanna leaves
granted two millennium of slumber
while Pharaohs passed to the land of the dead.
He seeks to abolish the ancient curse
of his people's enslavement.
He must find a special woman,
kiss the lips of his princess incarnate.
Along the way, his necrotic hands
with long pointed nails,
crush the heads of fanatics
bent to Allah in prayer.
Little do they know, this mummy
served as warrior to Amon-Ra
in the reign of Ankhenaten. The magic
of spells cast on sarcophagus
still control his movement.

Car bombs explode beside him,
insurgents shoot at him from rooftops,
and when the smoke clears,
he still limps along as before.
Nothing stands in his path,
he wipes away all before him
as he wends his way to the home
of a beautiful, veiled woman.
He rips away the door of the house,
lifts the veil from her face,
the wife of a suicide bomber, who screams
the same shrill screams
of her husband's bloody victims.

As he kisses her lips, hate melts away,
she opens her eyes to new light,
forgets night, time, and faith,
no longer judges or marks
division between people.

In ecstatic embrace, the two bodies
crack, crease, crust, and crumble
to the musty smell of natron and dust.
Soon two shadows dot the wall,
two gray moths flutter around
a lone gray candle in the night.

HOPE FOR RELIEF

Four days in a single cell apartment,
stuffy, hibernating under the covers,
warmed by synthetic hearth of thermostat,
buried by a micro-organism,
paltry I, obstinate and irascible,
afraid of absence or death,
wait for recovery in old winter sun.

Outside, grackles cling to the skeletal wisteria
which weaves about as if death will not come.
In spring these birds will take flight at the least noise.
From my bedroom window, I watch their big eyes.
I wonder what it must be like to live above ground,
make shoots, open pods, take flight.

ILLUSION

Motley pigeons perch on the picnic table,
their eyes widened at our presence.
You, sitting across from me, chase them off
then go back to your book.
Do you have a flower in the leaves?

I look at you with curious eyes:
I see a chest of thick round night.
Below, between the belly, I see a ring of sap.
You, the book, the table, each together

A part of the big maple,
Bark sewn together in smooth straight lines.
I see you, then I see a tree. I look again,

seek you out among the foliage,
but see the road, traffic, and wind blown leaves
as two men and a dog amble by.

YOUR WORST NIGHTMARE

After traveling through two states,
one cloudy, the next sun-swathed,
you arrive at the usual building,
open the door for another long day
at desk and terminal to build a world
fantastic and esoteric as empty space.
The lady at the desk greets you with a smile
and points the way to the stairs.
This time your office lies empty,
the furniture all gone. Someone tacked
a note on the wall: "Moved to another location."

Not long ago your home resembled this:
the food uneaten, the page unmarked,
the words unwritten, so many books
gone to dust by moths and mildew,
a pictureless frame on a bare wall,
an impression left in the rug
from an old piece of furniture,
a chair or couch perhaps
which sunk down on long dark nights.

Each day when you open the window,
too much gravity keeps you down.
You try to wake up at the beach
or at home, but smother your face
in the blanket, umbrella or bikini
(if only you could ever fit into one),
but no remedy seems to work.
You try to sort out all the clutter
but can never let go.

Instead, now, here, in this place,
the shape of nothing is a cup
observed for hours, waiting to be filled
though you know it never can be filled.
The blackness makes you forget
the cold flash stare of empty rooms:
cold for cold and wall for wall, as if somehow
you know the staring will not cease.

As you turn from these remnants,
what you expected to find now gone,
you hope the universe is kind.
You hope the lady at the desk,
an incarnation of that universe,
carbon-based and breathing oxygen,
will tell you where the occupants have gone,
but she only grunts half-syllables
as if her mouth forgot the shape of words.
You beat your brow and leave,
annoyed at finding only questions.

The alarm clock rings. You tap it off.
Was this vision a dream?
Touch your face, your hands to make sure.
Breathe, breathe. Time to get out of bed.
You rinse your mouth in the sink,
make pancakes stored in the fridge,
eat the pancakes, then get dressed,
brush your teeth and grab the keys to leave.

REPLY FROM A PROPHET

After reading Richard Wilbur's "Advice to a Prophet"

When I come, as soon I surely must, to the streets of the city,
tear-eyed from crying certain death,
proclaiming your impending fall, beseeching you
in your own name to have self-scorn,

I will not spare you words of war, their weapons and rage,
the long trails of heat that singe the mind;
your proud unflinching hearts will destroy your kind,
unable to prevent the coming age

When you shall cower from the death of the race.
Begin to dream this place without you,
the sun on fire, the leaves scarred and withered,
a stern look on the cracked stone's face.

I speak of earth's impending change. You conceive it not and laugh
about this silly thing, and know not to your cost
how all that lives you made decay,
the seas polluted and the vines crushed to soot.

How naive your view! You *could* believe it
if I told you that the yellow-tailed deer
and red mottled fox will vanish in a clearing,
the jay toss her deformed eggs and curl to die,

the great oak grow stunted and sere
will lose its grip, and every stream and river
lose its brassy brine, its shiny salmon
struck dead from poison. Wait till you exist without

the dolphin's play or the robin's return,
these things in which you see yourself
and turn your head away instead,
your muted call of nature forth dispelled.

You have spoken of the fear of time in the clear
mouth of courage, in which distilled
the crackling lotus of the atom killed
all you crave or wish to crave.

With great remorse I tell you the thorny rose
of your hearts shall prick, come reprimanding
your lofty life and long standing place on top
when the final pages of your chapter close.

PALM READING

The veins of a hand, the muscles and ridges —
how far back the palm marks go!
Before your birth. When your atoms
floated in space. Gestated in nebulae.
Once part of meteor, star, or planet.

The palm marks hold the key to your world,
behavior, moods, words, and deeds.
The hand guides you down the sidewalk
on the way home, takes you on vacation
to the edge of the earth, unimaginable
places years before impossible to reach.

When a baby, you stood in the sandbox
or on the edge of the surf at the beach
and had no way to know your destiny.
Later, when grown up, your hand
still revealed stories about the future:
days spent in numbing poverty,
work for dreams at a big company,
the expected route everyone took
up the ladder of success.

Now look at yourself in your hand,
palm marks faded, face begun to wrinkle,
smiles creased, thinning hair, forgetful brain,
molecules rearranged, transformed, become
another creature, a different set of organs
and slow moving body in pain, legs
weakened from so many years of pressure.

You slowly disintegrate like others
who go on about their lives
and quickly forget the questions
they asked the first day of school:
Why am I here? What's my purpose?
Will it all matter once I'm gone?
You, like them, from the beginning,
consumed the world around you.

Hold your hand to the light and see
what others expect of a proper life:
marriage, children, family, large house
with plenty of room and fireplace
to sit before and cuddle on cold nights.
You feel left out of this life, alone,
free to come and go as you please
with no one to question or answer.
You hold this picture both relief
and burden, blessing and curse.

When day is done, you come home,
turn on the kitchen stove to make tea
and play the radio loud, though in the house
you disturb other occupants who turn
their hands in a daily routine.

You know one day it will all be gone
and you will return to pure carbon,
hydrogen (the noble gases), the fire
to light the furnace of a luminous star
in a galaxy light years away.

SUN SPOTS

As she sits in the hospital bed,
she looks at sun spots on skin,
remembers lying on blankets,
feels the heat in the sand,
roar of ocean and sound of laughter,
brown boys chasing brown girls
who wear yellow glasses,
build brown castles, dig up
yellow stones with brown shovels,
lay a yellow wreath over starfish.

The same yellow rooms at home,
years later wallpaper yellow
soon stained newspaper brown,
like her yellow hospital room
where the yellow nurse wheeled her,
skin brown, sere and faded,
to a yellow operating table,
a doctor who radiates her
to kill the evil lurking there.

Next morning the yellow nurse
wheels her down the yellow hall,
into the yellow room,
left to recover on the yellow bed,
the brown color now a lighter hue,
smothered by yellow sheets.

She looks at the yellow bedpost,
at "Get well soon" sticky smilies
left by her smiling grandchild
who just arrived beach-brown.
Bald from treatment, she lifts
her head off the yellow pillow
and looks at the youthful skin.

She feels her body rise and fall
like a wave of light on the sea,
the great sweep across light fields,
across light time and shining beaches,
to the final, dirty brown island
in the center of the sun.

SOLAR NIGHT

*"To watch the solar eclipse on Christmas Day,
poke a hole in a piece of cardboard;
hold it to the light and watch the shadow.
You would be looking at a shadow or image
of the sun without damaging your eyes."*

—*E-mail message from a mother to her son.*

You begin to wonder about the eclipse
and the day of the eclipse. Why this day?
When the lord or lady, or shall we say
androgynous one, entered the world,
this cruel, angry, scheming, petty world.
Are people blind? Have they forgotten?
Their eyes not accustomed to focused light.

This year Bethlehem is silent. No tourists
visit the sacred spot. No merchants
sell icons, votive candles, saint's knuckles.
The icons feel lonely and neglected in a corner.
And no wonder: it is the day to mark
those foul misdeeds eclipsed in sin,
the day the sun became a dark yolk,
when people lost their heads and forgot
a thousand years of decay and rot,
being animal, yet above the animal.

Still, like everyone else, you wait patiently,
hoping clouds will not obscure the view.
You missed the event the last time around
and do not want to miss it again.
But why so special? This black egg yolk,
tadpole head, bride-veiled light?
Why now? Why at this hour of dire need,
the moment when the skeleton dances
in the window above the tinseled leaves?
Only on this fateful day will you know
why shadow baptizes fire and burns away the sun.

SONG TO IMAGINATION

Give me the clean, unspoiled word
whose rhyme and rhythm live
in the safety of skilled hands,
Shiva's double-gestured twists
that shape new windows of a world
scarcely noticed in a tear or kiss.

Give me the clear, unseen music,
one voice singing with slight twang,
plangent strings spread across a balcony
of bitter past mistakes and irony
resolved in discord and much pain,
final in all the strident harmony
to make itself at last rebound.

This one sound, one steady sound,
tragic in a Biblical, mythic voice,
rising from the stream or woods
on the notes of a thrush or a hawk;
ever-present perishing sound:
and last, not least, will we see it grow
one stalk from all the dying shoots?

Oh the transparent, naked vision!
without blemish, gimmick, or slogan,
like the upturned leaf upon whose veins
we see the microscopic lives that feed;
like the picture pure, serene in paint,
seen through speechless eyes,
spread by noble, nameless hands
across canvas caves of long ago.

Away with the base, muck and mire!
Climb the stairs to the highest cliff,
soar like a falcon to the crest,
and conquer dragons in the air.
Away from what lies beneath!
the animal and fierce desire.
Hold fast to shreds of the sublime!

Is there hope in a hateful din?
In the twin, twain confusing voice?
Music and painting all the same
hobble on old clichés and rhyme,
politics and ever-present race.
Beauty rests a decibel above
the world obscure and lame.

This world, the old word made new,
the flourish in the sound of brass,
the brush stroke and the fiery kiln,
bursts its way through noise and smoke
and makes us praise its name.

DOCTOR P.......

Of asphodels,
yachts
and broken bottles
he sings
from behind a green-glass
hospital wing,
where a red, gigantic, five-figured
fire truck rumbles
to destruction in the rain
which falls in the radon swamp,
on the hag's body
he tries to heal with medical pouch,
paraphernalia of poems
carried across the marsh
into the center of Passaic,
the locust tree that flowers
beneath the pink church
calling rebels from worship
into white sweet May again —
all in a Sheeler photo,
on the museum wall,
next to the exhibit of a red
dung-filled wheelbarrow.

NARRATIVE

FOUR VISIONS OF THE MUSE

I. The Maid

She creeps in the room on tiptoe
with submissive, furtive glances,
poem already in hand,
a sonnet about love.
"Put it there on the table!"
his voice peals with thunder.
Eyes never leave the newspaper,
as he puffs puffs puffs his pipe.
She puts the tray down, poem on dish
next to Chinese teapot, cup and fork,
with sheep smiles takes out duster,
gives his collar and shoulder a wipe.
He takes up the poem, opens his mouth,
puts it down, picks it up. "Oh my soul,
you are wondrous in my presence,
with your radiant garments and tits…"
he begins to read, puts it down,
then waves her away.
"That was so easy," he thinks.
She pours the tea from pot into cup,
leaves the pot on the tray,
vanishes from the room.

II. The Whore

The door creaks open. She enters,
flickers her tongue like a snake,
struts back and forth, jiggles her breasts,
rubs hands through hair and says:
"If you want the poem, search my body."
He gets up, strips off her clothes;
frenetic, he searches for it
like a badger burrows for food.
She tilts her head and laughs,
puckers her lips, arms round his neck,
as he pulls it from the cleavage
between her breasts. He smells it,
holds it up like a trophy,
reward for licentious toil.
He holds it up again, clears his throat
three times and begins to read:
"My wife is a bitch.
She peels onions on my arm.
I turn to my daughter and say,
'How bout a movie with daddy?'"
He stops, puts it down.
"It was so easy to rip this off."
She bends her behind in his face,
moans as he sticks it inside.
She crosses the room, turns her head,
flickers her tongue,
vanishes through the door.

III. The Hag

The door opens. In a wheelchair
comes a little old lady in rags.
Disheveled, warty, skin hangs
from beneath her chin.
Now fat and filmy-eyed,
successful beyond compare,
he walks over, shakes her by the hair:
"My love, bless me with laurel
and lyre in my final days.
Give me the gift of song.
I still don't know if what I write
is poetry or prose. I always thought
I could scream it out, slam it,
or scribble on the page,
crude jokes about missing fingers,
doggerel about families
and mundane lives."
Arthritic hands reach up
in tentative gesture. She tries
to form words with a wrinkled
mouth but only says, "Oh, oh,"
then falls back to the chair.
She drools, stares around the room,
at the geezer in the chair.
"Please, please," he beseeches.
She wheels herself, a race car
in slow motion, to rest at the door.
The door opens. The lady vanishes.

IV. Dame Death

Beard to the floor, in a creaky chair,
he looks up in final breath:
"I spent my life writing prose
that looked like poetry,
only to be famous. Now I want
the pure line of song."
A hooded dwarf draped in black
stands on a chair, sickle in hand,
looks down at him and smiles,
points to words on the page,
mouths as if reading a poem,
but only speaks silence.
When she slices the sheet in half,
he gasps and clutches his throat,
sinks with the shreds to the floor.
He grasps for the scraps,
hugs them close, tries to read
and form words, but is speechless.

Her skeletal hands reach out,
bony arms raise the sickle
and lower it in successive thrusts.

M.B.

The initials on my prison wall
Honor the mother who bore me.
I have no sorrow for the death I caused,
though it caused much grief for others.
When the robins nest three times,
I bid farewell to dishonored birth.

My mother and father courted
under falling cherry blossoms.
Years later my father returned
with a blond wife from abroad.
My mother met them at the gate
with a dagger thrust in her breast.
Father and his new wife cried
and claimed me as their own,
but I cursed them and forbade them
to raise me in their home.
He smacked me twice and cried,
"How dare he curse my blood!
May he live in sorrow all his life,
and may the sun never warm his face!"

Two courtiers gave me education
and raised me as their own.
I never loved them nor cared
to look upon their faces
as I slept sound in the garden.
Half of both races at once,
I knew little of race or country.
With slit wrists and slashed veins,
I cried for the parents who bore me.

All my wealth meant nothing;
nothing mattered but revenge.
Even to my lover, I brought grief,

regret, despair, and longing.
In the university we walked arm in arm,
then I pushed her aside and left her
sobbing in the garden.
When the robins nest three times,
I shall reclaim my lost lover.

Servants bore my father's life
in letters sent from overseas
and return address for his home.
I learned he fought in the Second Great War,
a decorated war hero.
I hated him all the more for this.
Baggage in hand, I boarded a flight
to the United States of America.
After my trip, I'd wash my hands
of his country and his memory.

I stumbled, lost my way, and found
the city of his second wife.
In the crepuscular glow of evening,
in a yard clean from debris,
pristine, as if sanctuary,
a pale, gray-haired woman
opened the door, stood on the stoop,
eyes all inquiry and wonder.

"Where is my father?" I asked,
standing in front of her.
 "Who are you?" she asked, eyebrows raised.
"What's wrong?" came a voice from inside.
A man in a wheelchair, war-bound,
rolled to the door, behind her.
I pushed his whore aside,
a ravaged rag doll,
and plunged my dagger in his heart!

TITHONUS IN MODERN TIMES, HUMAN AND GRASSHOPPER

I
Only yesterday, I lay in the park grass
counting the number of creatures,
arms outspread, overcome by the sun.
As darkness spread its shadow,
I nodded away my familiar world
till I saw grass blades the size of planets
and darted across the horizon
of gigantic trees and water.
When Dawn's spirit rose from the other side,
her pink fingers caressed me awake
to the gift of eternal life.
"My love, arise and be mine forever."
I embraced her and kissed her,
my fear dissolved in her arms,
virility a feeling eternal.
After a hundred years, I grew old and infirm.
She came to me in the morning,
fingers pink like a little girl's.
Tired of the many years of toil,
of long winters cold, dark, and brutal,
I begged her to end my sorrow,
the constant chill of death,
the inability to die.
Rather than take my life, in pity
she wrapped me in warm blankets
like a caterpillar in cocoon.

II
Terrified, for a second time I awoke,
With human mind and thought
in the body of another creature —
looked out from honeycombed eyes
on a bulbous head, opened a jaw
of mandibles, my body a plate of mail
on spiked, spindly, skeletal legs —
a bit like a bearded man in leather
glued to his Harley Davidson.
I went to move like the day before,
but hopped on four legs instead of two,
the hind legs larger and stronger,
bounced up and down on my back,
a feeling of constant hunger
propped me upright and forward.
I spread leathery wings and darted
like a bullet to the nearest tree.
The park appeared an immense sea
of green, the trees monolithic monsters
sent to crush me and my kind.
When I screamed or sang, strident sounds
issued from my scratchy throat.

Now each day I consume the grass
in which I once played ball —
an eternity of hunger unsated.
I chew holes in leaves people brush
on their walks through the forest.
Alone and apart from their world,
each of us equally alien, I am yet content
after all those years, after the first few moments
of sheer terror and utter madness.

I dwell apart from the world of my birth
and have no regrets for the loss,
among instead my fellow *Acrididae*,
a species millions of years old
who feed on the fresh summer grass
and crumbs left in the rain,
who lie dormant in the depths of snow
to awaken again with the warmth
of a spring sunrise.

MAIDEN TREE: A PASTORAL

I
In human form I often sat
on a blanket of forest leaves,
across the dandelion grass
where ants trembled on blade-tips,
and I watched the trickle of light
shine through webbed fingers
of Oaks above me.

I once went to the well for water,
for the dewgrass dipped in honey,
so the chickens and cows could drink,
so the thirsty mouths of my sisters
would lap and quench their lips
that lusted after blond, bright rays.

My sisters looked to me for wisdom
to repair the decrepit, stinking farm
broken by storms.
With our limbs taut and bent,
we looked to the sun for strength,
to his large, manly shoulders.

II

We dared to chase the sun
while in heat, while he went around,
dared to worship his coming and going
and to call him after he left.
Each time we enraged him more
in our courting and coyness
until one day he nearly caught us.
All but I escaped.

Then the sun sheared my flesh
and tore through ligaments,
my dress dangling in shreds.
I asked not to be chosen by a god,
to give my body without consent.
Instead, he punished me for flirting.

III

The voice of my mother earth
and shock of my brother moon
wailed over laughter of uncle sun
after he raped me.
Then I no longer wished for light
but to blot out my eyes with a pin.

Henceforth I loathed human affection
and shunned all human touch,
the brown hands of the nymphs, my sisters,
who wept each time they passed the well
and saw me shriveled and dying,
skin wrinkled like an old crone's.

IV

When father river saw me thus,
he turned me into an oak tree,
my fingertips sprouting leaves,
thick branches hanging down,
shingled and brown,
corrugated bark gnarled and sere.

Now I can only stand immobile
among sisters who wonder,
as for centuries others stood
and watched leaves blossom, then sever.
Daily I endure the sun's golden darts,

Then rain, sleet and snow
a part of spinning seasons.
I can only watch and wait for death:
slimy slugs who slide up my sides
and grubs who gnaw my roots,
those fungoid tentacles spread to engulf
teeming life under the earth.

V

Rooted in my mother's blood,
clinging to the folds of her skin,
I watch as eons pass: the farm
no longer a farm, my sisters
long swallowed by mother's body.
Other women with sisters' eyes
now seek a fetid hole for water.

Asphalt and a golf course
replace the verdant farm,
and cars run over the cows
who sit too long in the grass.

Wires extend webwork above
the growth of my pine friends,
where birds now screech
for want of abundant food.

Through changes of industrial man,
I can only stand and watch and pray
no blade slices me like an apple.
Hated by humans, I have protection
of uncle sun, whose light blinds
and scorches the human foe
once loved and admired as kin,
now my betrayers.

VI

I scatter acorns though few survive.
Most are eaten by squirrels or birds
who crack my fruit, however bitter.
The more gnarled and knotted I am,
the more attractive I become
to a song sparrow or woodpecker
who wants to make a home
in a harbor of leaves and branches
or in a hole in my side.

Who knows? As a tree,
I will live a thousand years,
then become a fossil,
stump locked in museum glass.
At least I'll be preserved forever
in my own dried sap.
Even dead remnants will endure
beyond mutable human flesh.

MONSTER'S REVENGE

One day on a walk by the river,
I think of him on the bottom.
Older than natives who bathed on the banks,
who feared him and left gifts.
Older than the river before the water rose.
I listen to the water lap the shore
and imagine he begins to stir in anger
from accumulated plastic, rubber and silicon,
needles and syringes.

He comes in the beaked night,
in the growl unleashed from the belly.
Wading slowly, head first, then lips,
chin and neck, beard crusted like shale
into the folds of his chest.
Plastic cups hang from his body,
beer bottles hang from his neck,
talismans or trophies of the hunt.

He licks his lips from river brine,
Salivates for arm or leg, burps
with odor of slug after dirty rain.
Grime crawls on his hairy body,
a wreath of mud cakes his eyes.
I know he has come to reclaim
the mangled world once his:
Marsh, twig, stone and scarred tree.

Mistaken for Gillman if viewed
from afar, icicles crumple the hair
of his body and crunch as he walks
on a Sunday stroll though the park,
across the frozen football field and path
out to the street where a driver yells
"Look where you're going asshole!"
He would snap the driver's neck in two
if he could catch the car.
He reaches for the car as it passes.

A line of slime trailing behind,
he walks up two blocks and one over,
sees more cars and frightful stares,
reaches my house, thumps on the door,
bear claws scratching wood grains.
I point to the door of the landlord,
watch him shatter it, hear screams inside,
as I wipe the slime from my hands.

FOOTPRINTS

At night I come in from fallen snow
behind the door and beyond.
Footprints, embedded in sidewalk,
pass through strange lands
where herds of animals climb metal mountains.

Each day my feet journey to a childhood home
far from usual habitations.
as if concealed in special confinement,
voices and feet on stairs
drown in echo-chamber hallways,

While beyond the wall,
outside,
a child playing in the street
calls for home and its mother,
everywhere and nowhere.

In the house dead ancestors,
who once greeted me from behind curtains,
glide around solitary rooms
to the exact spot their feet once stood,
then go out the door and beyond —

This permanent residence my own
but never inhabited,
except as a child knowing nothing —
only the sound of my own voice
echoed in the hallway.

After leaving home, I dream
a botched escape from an ancient cell,
the road opening into darkness. Along the way,
strangers look out through husks once eyes.
Their feet leave only bird prints in snow.

I look for the origin of footprints,
sound of sea surf smashing against snowy rocks,
along the edge of railroad tracks
stretching into the long cold night.

From my room I peer into darkness
for a sign from the god of footprints.

LOSS

What I liked about it was the way it wiggled over the top of the refrigerator, moving slowly like a slug, breathing heavily, sighing;

and I liked that it spoke of freedom to chart my own life, like the clock sucking blood out of each moment of feeling;

and every winter morning at six when I got up to wash the scum from my mouth, I looked into the mirror and came to terms with my own grief.

And what they, those false parents, didn't know about it was that I ate it every morning for breakfast, in place of egg or toast.

And what they didn't know about it was that it held me in its grasp and looked into my eyes before leaving the house.

And what they never knew was how often I left home, walked down the street, crossed traffic and kept walking to disappear and get lost in the next town, where I could find what I had lost;

and what they still don't know is how each day I keep killing the slugs and clocks that invade my home, and that each day I perform this ritual;

and what they still don't know is how I wear the dead clocks and slugs around my neck as a talisman to remind me of the grief left behind in people I know, real parents and friends forgotten or gone;

to ward off buried fear, ward off the brown color that invades my home, the sense of no one and nobody and the nothing in the garden.

It is that continual loss which can't be controlled.

DEADPAN ALLEY

So another night alone, so soon come and gone. Need love, to linger with new woman just born out of sight and sound. And so to a marvelous, tree-filled, fountain-fed café on the edge of town where shoes sit still and who knows what childish person lurks just below the water? Who knows what acrobats have fiendish designs or passageways to another world, inside where everything grows, silence and amplification of soundness, soundless. Whose sound? Hush! Make no sound. Without a word a bird chirps. A bug shouts.

Aware am I of language and desire for connection with tree, rock, animal, bird, break-out of cage, cave, hole in the center and move outward toward another center around the window where I write words about the window and eyes in the window. And so it flows: language, music, crickets, bugs, birds, windsong in dry night and cool flesh of god on thigh. Almost too late toward midnight to forget the night before when shouts and clown shows ruled the atmosphere in tree-laden coffee shop. So I write after calling for space of cage, using it up, making the worst of it, past window beyond outside into woman wearing curly wig, bra, stockings, garters, jeans, bushy socks and shoes of earth, dark woman dressed like night.

NONSENSICAL

SINGER

I live inside an airtight world
that never sings to me.
Sounds that flow outside its lung
wheeze gently out to sea.
The dreary days, the sunny days,
what matters if they fall?
I work hard or not at all
to kiss the city lake of glass
and cross the scaly carpet stone
unfurled and glued along the grass.
The vision comes in walks I take,
it matters not to me.
My world's compressed into a ball
each time I turn to see
the black descending pallid pall
that always floats away,
like silence in the room I eat
with all three meals a day.
A cynic's mood comes over me,
I gasp at all the ghosts I see,
who haunt the bodies I have known,
the smiles and eyes now gone,
for they will never greet again
and I will always be alone.

SKYFALL

The businessman walks home without a plan.
He does not know he ever can
come and go at will.
Still, he eats the ancient krill
that wander in the shadows of his mind.
Like spoons beaten on the rear of melon rind,
he hardly makes a look or glance
toward tree or bird to give him trance.
If the sky falls it falls by chance.

He does not know he ever can or ever will
come and go in shadows of his mind
beaten on the end of melon rind,
like spoons apportion out a look or glance
at tree, bird, root or lance,
lovers like him without a plan.
He eats his kill in ancient night.
If the sky falls it falls by chance.

Still, he siphons out his soul on ends of spoons,
forged only in the shadows of his mind,
the space between the shadows and the rind,
the plan and lack of plan,
of melon casting look or glance
at half-moon demon lovers in a trance
that keeps them whirling in the noon.
If the sky falls it falls by chance.

LAMENT IN SUMMER

I'll be in paradise by six o'clock.
I'll take the next train out of town
and work all day until I drop,
until fatigue rattles my bones,
penetrates my limbs, and surly
I arrive at home and take a flop.

I'll take the next train out of town,
past the fast food and its dire smells,
past the movies with useless images,
women sitting on porches in the sun,
until fatigue rattles my bones
and penetrates my surly limbs
which flop in bed upon arrival home.

I'll work all day until I drop,
until I can no longer breathe but choke
on my picture in the local paper
that stands still in time, out of light,
under shaded trees to cover me
as shrouds cover children who are dead.
I'll study how it penetrates my limbs
and makes me take a drop in bed.

I'll be in paradise by six o'clock
When fatigue rattles my bones, whose marrow
empties like the yolk sucked out of egg,
as when I take a walk down town
and see how movies come and go,
how lovers wrap themselves like sandwiches
then blow away like cardboard in the wind.

I feel like them when on the train,
when making my escape to double feature,
past the women, the signs, the Kmart stores,
all the marks of what's called civilized.
I'll be in paradise by six o'clock

When I'll curl in discarded images
of women sitting on porches in the sun
and fall away into the shrouded bed,
the final shadows of incessant dead.

DAY AT THE CIRCUS

Hyenas jeer at the clown
who smiles with a frown
because they do not understand
he is king of juggling,
his tightrope his own making,
and tigers from which he runs
are pages that he gives a name.

He is the poetaster of the sea,
ventriloquist of conch,
gap-jawed, rag-tagged travesty,
prestidigitator par excellence,
allegorical alligator of renown,
the reptilian service man of nonce,
the only one who apes in town,
who juggles space upside-down.

As politician of planets and their motions,
he plucks the strings that makes things go,
gives a pattern to the constellations
and brings to mortals weal or woe,
or so the superstitious clods believe
who look to false gods for answers to their pain.

Hyenas jeer at the clown
who smiles with a frown
as he bounces up and down
upon his broken crown.

This Parmenides of comic cosmic dust
alchemizes metal into rust
like King Midas with a rotten touch.
As much a weapon as a toy,
he conquers illusion with a blow.

Watch him as he makes his rounds
past animals caged in zoos,
each one resembling human form
trapped in a prison of its choosing.

Hyenas jeer at the clown
who smiles with a frown
but with ignorance they forget
how he leads them on a string
in the center of the ring.

See him ride the ghostly garbage truck
and dump the trash from mental cans
that inhibit and keep a body buried,
from growing like him into a clown.

Yet in his surreptitiousness and stealth,
from here to there and back again,
he reveals all in nothing but himself:
a Pandora who jumps out from the box.

HURDY-GURDY

One day in church the hurdy-gurdy man
grinds gypsy tunes from long ago that weep.
An invisible monkey runs to and fro
astride big arms, shoulders, and his feet.
He cranks the music high and low
as if a voice speaks in his stead
of why we gather in the room
to celebrate the chemistry of star,
the killing of a fly by a spider's grasp,
the origin of lion's roar.

The hurdy-gurdy, nothing more
than gypsy dance on moonless nights
creeps under skin, raises hair of doubt
to question why this mortal frame persists
and perseveres despite contrary odds,
propensity to vain and hasty thought.
The answers come in pages told
of frogs to children during story time,
how they lost dominion over lairs of snakes,
and the trees who shed leathery leaves
let go of life again as in the past.

The hurdy-gurdy plays the ancient theme
upon its guttural clanking keys,
the man who plays it never knowing why,
only that he came this day
to draw the canvas of the universe
upon the fingers' sound and touch,
while a wild, imaginary monkey
raises brows, gapes, and runs away.

PHANTOM

It sneaks around the corner,
Grabs you in the theater,
Peaks at you from bathroom stall,
Hides inside the nearest mall,
Makes you thirsty, tired,
Comes across the outer wall
And takes away utensils mired
In the basin of your sink.
It's quick to scalp you with a wink!

This monster knows no remorse.
It will make you stay the course
Into oblivion and beyond,
Into the time you can't pay bills,
The time you can't write wills
Because it's written you must pay,
You must give your life away
Without consent, vote or confidence!

Yes, the phantom looms
In each corner of your rooms,
Its hand reaches for your face,
Your house, your car, your shoes.
It will drag you to disgrace
By hair of head or underwear.
It cares not what you lose,
How obtained, how forgotten,
It makes your food turn rotten,
Makes you vomit on your plate.
This monster is the State!

TO POETS WHO WOULD BE FASTIDIOUS

You clear away the tablecloth
And wipe away the crumbs,
And hide the mats for dishes
When guests announce they'll come.

"I need to comb my hair"
You say and rush around the room,
Bite your nails and scratch your face
And hope nobody comes.

Perhaps tuxedo fits you well
Or shirt with tie and starched collar

Worn for simple folk who hardly know
A book, opera or show,
Or hardly care or dare to risk
A thing confusing, dark or ugly.

You turn and wait, turn and wait
And see yourself again:

Hair hanging down or cropped too short,
The lipstick not sensuous enough,
Your nails, the dirt behind the ears,
The crumbs on table, the salt that spilled.

FRAGMENT

During cold wind
What reason keeps me stagnant?
Like soil anticipating growth
The whole town leaps up
In impish clawed depravity.

As if sick in head or chest
A friend looks away in silence
And fears making the disease worse.
No reason keeps love unspoken
Except a head, cold
From too much mechanical labor.

Acute sunlight in fallen leaves
Weakness felt in empty stomach
Attempt and failure to change
A fevered world teeming larger daily.

In the open door only in the open door
One finds what lurks beyond the cold.
To kill infection a woman far away
Shakes a gourd in my direction.

In sunrise not in distracting rain
Streets shine brighter and cleaner.

POLITICAL

COMPANY KNEE

A patient looks out the hospital window
as the scene unfolds in a blur:
chopper's dragonfly descent
through shrapnel, bullets, grenades,
hit by a missile, out of control,
parachute dive into cliffs,
the rush across the field
of evaporated faces,
the knee sliced as he runs.

His eyes fade back into view
as he walks with a knee
through doors and hallways,
the stump from the war now gone,
such a good job he can't tell
the knee ever sliced like steak.
The new one came assembled,
seized from the field and glued
like a toy together,
plastic and metal added later.

Bored, the patient thumbs through the paper
and reads, *The company expects to bolster
Stabilizer Knees and heavily target
the military surgeon market.*
In the picture a designer with twisted face
holds up a thigh, a caption
he imagines with a sinister accent:
"Zis is human thigh bone. You must glue
to replace ze knee."

He throws down the paper,
turns on the television —
*The bombing will continue
until all refugees return home...*

The patient opens hospital doors
and walks into the light.
He remembers how, in the field,
a dog licked his knee clean
just after it severed, after
the carnage, the raping, the push
to become victor, to succeed
regardless of consequence.

LAST RITES

I sing the song of the wailing mothers
under the hands of a brute,
a bully, a pestilence on earth,
who silenced by sealing mouths shut;

the voices who crow like a bugle of war,
the orders given, the soldiers who march,
the tanks which move, the guns deployed,
the bullets which fly, the bombs dropped,

The heads hacked off,
held up for the world to see
as revenge for killing their own—

I embrace all. I am the people bombed
and the bombs dropped on people,
the adrenalin pumping fear,
the soil stained red,
and the blood in the raindrops.

I am the mullahs and holy men,
and I am the people who worship them.
I am the victims who scream in pain,
and the dictator who crushes his victims.
I am the soldier who in fear
makes prisoners kneel.
I am the prisoner who cries out,
humiliated and shamed.

I am the ears, eyes, and genitals
of the brave who went swiftly under
and never had time to say farewell
to people they loved at home.

I speak with their voices, vicarious, undaunted!
I hail them and give them last rites,
I sprinkle holy water on their souls
from Potomac to Euphrates alike.

I give them safe passage across the river
In my skull cap and rundown ferry
To the shore where nobody questions them,
Where they can rest at last content
And recover from the journey.

FEARS OF SORCERERS SPUR KILLINGS IN JAVA (INDONESIA)*

"Allahu Akbar!"
God is Great!

The police in Indonesia cannot stop
citizens from parading on bamboo stakes
the heads of people believed to be sorcerers,
who supposedly walk through town as black-
garbed rapid motion artists of concealment,
also called ninjas, not like the green toy turtles
every child knows and loves,
but people who are "different" in some way.

The police watch, in modern Indonesia,
as the citizens chop off heads of the ninjas
who before this
sat watching their wives giving birth,
or screamed in the arms of a sick loved-one.
Vigilantes roam the town looking for ninjas,
for the mentally disturbed who can't explain
a purpose for being, in the wrong place
at the wrong time.

Some ninjas vanish when attacked,
so the story goes from the locals,
others turn into cats, having just come
from a domestic life of chores
where cats breed by the hundreds.
Still others, when attacked in the night,
turn and stare in the glare of the floodlight
of interrogation. They cannot run and hide
as their captors can.
Vigilantes cut off their heads with machetes
as a way to avenge the deaths

among the Nadhdlatul Ulama,
Muslims assassinated in their sleep
near the resort of Bali.

But now if ninjas flee, they must be ninjas;
if they attack when cornered, they must be ninjas.
Like witches who were witches if they burned
and witches if they didn't, who were witches
if they drowned and witches if they didn't,
ninjas cannot escape justice
in modern Indonesia, whose police are afraid
of interfering out of fear vigilantes
will mistake *them* for ninjas
and cut off their heads with machetes.

"*Allahu Akbar!*"
God is Great!

---

*Derived from a *New York Times* article of same title.

AMOROUS

SUZETTE

It was a special day of cherries,
that day I saw the naked statue
of a Mayan goddess on a hill;
it was the day even Picasso's twisted bodies
grew breasts as round and firm as pineapples.
As we walked down the corridor together,
a voice echoed faintly but true
"It is time to practice arpeggios,"
and the bell tolled once as we passed by
a man resembling Adam blushing in the bushes.

It was a plumaged season, aqua winter,
pale, pale forehead, rose cheeks, rose on the cheeks,
lips pressed like petals on the face, nose full and round,
the smile of a cherub singing silently.
Sunday was a day of rest,
soft pear, wet orange, juicy apple, tart grapefruit,
flowing lines of a poem that is ceaseless,
surrounded by the towering colonnades
of a thousand songs yet unsung,
a thousand lovers seeking lost Eurydices.

Peacocks filled the museum.
Violins stretched tones of legs and thighs
on the coffee table, next to fluttering windows
where Frida Kahlo's face loomed
over the speck called being; each minute
strummed by every silent *fa* or *la*
could not match the pleasure spent with you.
Alas, my poor soul yearns for silence,
which you bring to me with every glance,
every sigh that is not language but is love.

CHINA DOLL

Like the wrapping of thread
around a dowel of wood,
you wrap yourself around me,
threads of silk on your arms
as your fingers play with my hair.
Your bent brow speaks to travelers
of clothes sold in a sweaty shop,
your days and nights alone and tired,
broken from lack of affection.
You help me select the best bargain
of shirts, pants, socks, and pajamas
from a storehouse of experience,
a shred of joy woven by hand
into the pattern of your face.
Night after night of rapture
speaks louder than a thought,
a kiss more content than a verb:
your polished skin and jade eyes
deeper than words ever go.
Soon we will no longer love,
separated by the great divide
of vast oceans and many lands.
I will carry you in pictures,
souvenirs, and mementos
across six thousand miles,
six thousand years of culture,
to reach my native land.
There you will live in dreams
of dragons, bats, butterflies,
a little doll in a corner shop.

ROSA

Round-nosed, plump, you wrap around, enclose me.
Not a prison for my soul but a protection,
A sanctuary and home away from home.
Brown native smell, sweet voice, smiling face,
Always the smiles even in the midst of despair.
Tame on the surface with your sighs
But underneath a wild animal.
A Mayan priestess or a Spanish nun?

Cortez abducted your culture but returned Spanish
And a Savior, the word for God, and gave me you,
The word inside my heart, the flesh and bone,
A creed needing no utterance or affirmation
Beyond words and their mortal prison.

From different worlds, we come together
Each time we share our company and food.
Like a communion of saints
Who share the same meal worlds apart,
Tortillas and tea instead of bread and wine,
Transubstantiation of old into new before the time
White-faced men like me took to ships for glory.

Our two natures mingle like genes of different roses
Or species of Mendel's pea,
The only difference one of color, shade, and shape,
The stuff of matter in essence the same,
The coupling of the urban and urbane
To make sense of why we two,
So different, so alike, yet love.

LOVE SONG

Outside the window, cold leaves flap into the forgotten shape of a bird, butterfly or beetle. The former warmth now gone, you and I seek an inner warmth not found outside.

You stand in the waning autumn light, your pale face attracting my desire for your love.

At once the wings of the beetle descend for the kill, broken then repaired like the illusion of water in hollow stone. The wings fly into the shape of a heart—the butterscotch of your sweet hair shining in the light, soon to be your lips.

We go together to different places, we seek different emotional spaces where we can come to love each other.

We rise, we sleep, we come, we go like the sky that ever-changes, like eyes that glitter ultraviolet, the spirit.

We seek connection, to understand each other without question, with full knowledge of the good, the bad, and the ugly.

In your presence I shudder like a hesitant hummingbird before an unbroken flower crowned with thorns, before the last breath of the sea or melting brook.

Alone, my tattered feathers feel limp and shiver in winter pain. But together, we flicker like angels in expiring flame.

IF I HAVE LOVE

My lover will be a warm coin in the pocket,
remnants of fresh coffee in the cup,
last shred of rain in afternoon shower,
the bookshelf and all the books unread,
museums with statues and winding staircases,
the drained face noticed in a faraway crowd,
a simple glance, smile, nod or greeting,
breath left on the window just before sunset,
moth flickering in light, silhouette and shadow,
a sanctuary and the penitent in prayer,
a finger or hand that draws forth tears,
the body held when nothing is left to hold,
the last person in the room who,
changing and changeless,
stays and never looks back.

PINEAPPLE LOVERS

They open refrigerator door, twist
a can of pineapple rings, each piece
thrown in the air to sprinkle
and fall on their naked bodies.

Each in the other's arms, they waltz
to memory of childhood summer,
round and round on the carousel
as they try to catch the yellow ring.

They spin from room to room,
to the bathroom, to the shower
of pineapple juice, whose yellow soap
caresses the body, seeps into pores.

As they step from the shower,
their bodies gleam in rings of sunlight.

LOVE LANGUAGE

I go to work each day to teach
a way to speak, to listen, and to read
the signs and symbols of a world
where people young and old alike
struggle with a language of their own.

Like them, I often find myself alone
in my life where love's a void
without touch from man or woman,
the language never tried nor true,
its practice never acted out on stage.

It's difficult to read the signs, no doubt,
that speak of bonds between two souls
because I never took a course in passion,
never found the time to work for love,
but stayed at home and studied solitude.

And now the mass of stars and planets
spin round and round with no consolation.
The many constellations grow no love
nor give the hungry soul satisfaction.
Thus life continues in an empty fashion.

Death will do its part to keep a wall
between the fate of one man at a table
and the person soon to be his partner:
man or woman, it makes no difference
when the body turns to dust and ashes.

ONCE LOVED

Just imagine what it's like
to never feel lurid fingers prick
the fluid of the central chord
attached to brain and neurons
who fire off and sing in seconds
the feeling against skin,
a kiss on lips but once.

Has one ever, while in Venice,
stood on a parapet looking down
at failed attempts to embrace
strangers walking in a crowd
together, their children a parody
multiplied as in a prism?

Will there only once
be a fatal, heart-stopping kiss
even from the lips of a confidant;
arms, fingers, hands around
cosmography of hips
circumnavigated
like a strange new world?
Will youth gather in the end,
go forth by day, look into the light,
a safer place of bones forgotten?

All mail sent and left unopened,
words by students left unspoken,
sailors who leapt toward the light,
mean nothing without the sound
of a familiar's voice, adoration
of a vision held in sunset arms
from atop Venetian tower,
then released in balance battle,
forgotten in the fall to water.

As others led astray find anchor,
so the faithful mariner at port of call
finds comfort in the living fluid
and solace in a face.

WHEN OPENING THE BOOK, YOU WILL SEE THIS:

Love is written on the heart, not on stone
of the mountain chiseled rough by Time
who ravages the salty sea to bone.
Only the heart reflects the lover's face,
a certain look or nod, a touch or kiss
despite the demons seeking to unseat.

Of the mountain only the heart knows
when cast into the sea by angry fate,
how the cello's and the whale's song
stretch across both time and space,
how a certain look or nod restores the bliss
grown wiser when chiseled rough
by demons of the mind.

He who ravages the salty stone to dust
knows not the mountain cast into the sea,
Time chiseling away dour demons
who burn a hole in the blanket of a kiss.
Only the universe reflects the lover's eyes
in billion-year-old light, the heart engulfed
by the fiery tongue of fate.

The same heart hewn on rough sea cone
knows the law written in the book of fate,
the key to unlock the tentative face,
a hand of pity and a fatal kiss
that leads down, down, down
into oblivion and the underworld below.

ABOUT THE AUTHOR

Thomas D. Jones' first book of poetry, *Genealogy X*, was published by The Poet's Press in 2000. His poem "Flute Girl" appeared in *Language and Culture* (online) in the Winter of 2008 and his poem "A Bagger's Life" appear in an anthology called *Appleseeds* in Fall 2008. His poetry last appeared in *Raintiger* (raintiger.com), *The Surface*, *Scrivener's Pen* and *Write-Away* on-line journals, and his work has been published in numerous print magazines throughout the country.

Originally from northern New Jersey, he has a BA in English and an MA in Publishing Studies from New York University, and is the former publisher and poetry editor of *Wings*, an online magazine. After twelve years in the publishing field in the New York/ New Jersey area, he began teaching ESL and computer skills at adult education programs in Rhode Island, and is now a mail clerk at the United States Postal Service.

www.ingramcontent.com/pod-product-compliance
Lightning Source LLC
Chambersburg PA
CBHW051655040426
42446CB00009B/1156